The Jack of All Trades

...Master the Back Office and Turn Pitfalls into Profits!

Many small business owners are drowning in the paperwork of daily tasks while doing it all themselves. They soon recognize that they are wearing many hats by having to navigate all of the tasks inherent in the BACK OFFICE, which include understanding taxes, payroll, insurance, legal, accounting, cash flow, and financial management, etc.

Small business owners, entrepreneurs and leaders must quickly learn how to delegate many of these tasks while still maintaining responsibility for the outcome. Are you in control of your business?

In this Itty Bitty Book®, Karen O'Connor will share with you 15 simple tips to guide you through your Back Office.

How to structure your business to protect your personal assets and minimize your tax liability.

- How to leverage business credit and debt to increase cash flow and grow your business.
- How to protect your business from cyber threats.

Pick up a copy of this powerful book today and begin building a solid foundation for success!

Your Amazing
Itty Bitty®
Mastering
The Back Office
Book

15 Simple Tips to Build a Successful
Business From Inside the Back Office

Karen O'Connor, MBA

Published by Itty Bitty® Publishing
A subsidiary of S & P Productions, Inc.

Printed in the United States of America

Itty Bitty® Publishing
311 Main Street, Suite D
El Segundo, CA 90245
(310) 640-8885

ISBN: 978-1-931191-08-1

Dedicated to Mike and Colton. Love you guys!

Stop by our Itty Bitty® website to find interesting blog entries regarding Back Office Tips and Information.

www.IttyBittyPublishing.com

Or visit my website at
BackOfficeTips.com

Table of Contents

Introduction – Jack of All Trades

Introduction
Jack of All Trades
Mastering the Back Office

In this Itty Bitty® Book you will find simple tools, tips and tricks for operating your business. As a business owner, you will wear many hats and perform many roles.

The **Back Office** is the operations center or hub of your business. Dealing with paperwork, bookkeeping, bankers, vendors, employees, customers, taxes, etc., is not always exciting or fun, but it is essential in creating a sustainable foundation for success. Identifying the different roles and responsibilities and creating systems and procedures will save you time, money and energy.

DIY (Do It Yourself) Entrepreneurs must quickly learn how to delegate or outsource many of these tasks without abdicating control or responsibility. The goal is to empower small business owners to pursue their dreams by providing simple, reliable, trustworthy Back Office solutions.

This book will provide you with a general overview of the many departments, roles and responsibilities of your business. It is intended to familiarize you with the required vocabulary necessary to ask the right questions and to seek expert guidance, whether from your CPA, bookkeeper, banker or attorney. Use this book as a resource guide. Refer back to it often and keep yourself on the path to success.

Tip 1
To Be or Not To Be
What Entity Shall I Be?

Whether you are starting a new business or operating an existing business, understanding the different types of entities is a key step to building a rock solid foundation. Selecting the right structure for your business can minimize taxes and protect your ass (assets).

1. Sole proprietorship: Simple, cheap and easy to set up. No asset protection and fewer tax breaks. There is no separation between you and your business.
2. Partnership: Same as above, but with more people and opinions.
3. Limited Liability Company (LLC): Easy to set up, formed through the state, provides asset protection and limits liability. Some states allow one member.
4. C-Corporation and S-Corporation.
   a. Must file with Secretary of State.
   b. Requires stricter compliance procedures.
   c. Provides liability and asset protection.
   d. Increased tax advantages.
   e. Requires a higher level of recordkeeping for compliance with IRS.
   f. S-Corps are pass-through entities (do not pay taxes) and C-Corps are separate taxable entities.

Piercing the Corporate Veil.
My Alter Ego Made Me Do It!

When a corporation or LLC is overshadowed by an individual and the entity fails to separate itself from the transactions of that individual, it is referred to as the individual's **ALTER EGO**. If a company fails to conduct business under the proper corporate formalities, a court or the IRS could find the shareholder(s) or member(s) personally liable for the obligations and debts of the company. You must maintain clear separation!

- The company is a separate legal entity with its own TIN (tax identification number).
- You must maintain corporate formalities such as: observing bylaws, operating agreements, corporate minutes, separate recordkeeping, maintaining company in good standing, compliance with state and federal requirements.
- You must have sufficient capital to meet the business operations and obligations.
- No comingling of business and personal expenses, assets or liabilities.
- Sole shareholder corporations are still required to hold board meetings and shareholder meetings. As the lone attendee, document all the positions you hold and clearly outline the discussion and outcome of the meetings.

Tip 2
Paperwork
The Necessary Evil

Tedious, boring, dreadful, time consuming –
UGH! Handling and processing paperwork is
essential to understanding the financial position
and profitability of your business. It supports
your tax deductions, saves you money on taxes,
qualifies you for lower interest rates and
insurance premiums, keeps you out of trouble
with the IRS and can protect you from frivolous
lawsuits. Simple!

1. Deal with paperwork the first time you touch
    it. Saves you time, money and energy.
2. Save ALL DOCUMENTS that have to do
    with your business: receipts, bills, invoices,
    bank statements, etc.
3. Document the date, amount, description,
    purpose and how it was paid or received.
4. KEEP ALL RECEIPTS. At minimum, keep
    in a shoebox. At least you have them.
5. Create a filing system that works for you.
    Can you find it when you need it and can
    someone else find it when you can't
    remember!
6. Do not commingle personal and business
    transactions. Maintain separate checking
    accounts and credit cards.

Keeping Records

- Income Tax Returns with supporting documents: 3-7 years.
- Employment Tax Records: 4 years.
- Business Asset Records: Keep as long as you hold the property. Hold additional 3-7 years after disposal. Records will show basis, depreciation, amortization and any gains or losses.
- Business documents such as corporate meetings and minutes, annual reports, by-laws, amendments, stock ledgers, formation documents, etc.: Permanently.
- Payroll Records and Human Resource Files: 7 years.
- Cancelled checks, bank account and credit card statements: 7 years or longer if for tax purposes.
- Business ledgers, journal entries, check registers, Profit & Loss Statements (P&L), and other financial reports: Permanently.
- Finally, if the paper clutter is too much, scan and store in the cloud. Remember, always have a backup.

"In this world nothing can be said to be certain, except death and taxes."
~Benjamin Franklin

Tip 3
Choosing Your Accounting System
Not Too Big, Not Too Small, But Just Right

Most basic accounting programs include: income and expense tracking, bank reconciliation, invoicing and financial reporting. The first step in choosing your accounting software is to ask yourself a few questions:

1. WHAT do you need the accounting software to do: asset management, inventory, manage customers, job costing, project management, financial analysis, budgeting, etc.?
2. How much of an investment in time and money are you willing to make?
3. Will you need to do your own payroll or will you outsource this function to a professional payroll service?
4. Will you be learning the software yourself or do you need an experienced bookkeeper?
5. Will you get the reports you need to make critical financial decisions?
6. Will the software keep pace with the growth and needs of your company?
7. Do you understand the pros and cons of a cloud system vs. traditional desktop version?
8. Talk to other businesses in your specific industry. What software are they using? What do they like and dislike about it?

Accounting Software

- Recommendations are important. Do not base your decision solely on a software sales person. They may not be able to clearly understand the idiosyncrasies of your business.
- While the role of your accountant is important, their recommendation may be biased toward the accounting systems they know and use and not what you need.
- Your accounting software can do more than just keep the books. It is a data base!
- An accounting program is an investment in both your time and money. Who will be the one learning, processing and preparing the reports that you will ultimately rely on for financial decisions and tax preparation?
- Using accounting software does not make you a bookkeeper or accountant. It is simply a tool to process and streamline your financial data.
- Finally, beware of GIGO (garbage in, garbage out). Your accounting program does not know or care if the information being processed is correct or not. That is up to you!

"Everything should be made as simple as possible, but not simpler."
~Albert Einstein

Tip 4
The Game of Hide and Seek

Without sales of your product or service, it does not matter how good your recordkeeping is, how well your accounting program works or what tax structure you are. You need to find customers that want to buy your product or service. This requires research, planning and creativity to develop a marketing strategy to align the two.

1. Target your market. Be specific. The money is in the niches.
2. Use market research and demographics to find your ideal Customer Avatar.
3. Have the customer mindset. Put yourself in the customer's shoes.
4. GOOGLE it. Is anyone searching for it? Any paid advertisers (see Google/Facebook Ads)?
5. Are you solving a particular problem?
6. Differentiate from the competition.
7. Provide more benefits, increase value.
8. Provide a guarantee.
9. What is your USP – Unique Selling Point?
10. Provide exceptional customer service.
11. Package or bundle products and services.
12. Ask for feedback from your customers.
13. Ask for referrals. Cheap and effective.
14. Become the expert. Give out GOOD and FREE information. Become a TRUSTED source. Who will they call first?

Managing Customer Expectation

- Retaining current customers is far more cost effective than finding new ones.
- Develop cash incentives, discounts, rewards and referral programs.
- Happy customers and their word of mouth is the best form of advertising.
- Take responsibility for the situation or problem. The customer is only interested in hearing about a solution and how it is going to benefit them.
- Never make excuses. This shifts fault away from you and onto your customer.
- Use discounts wisely. This can devalue your brand, product and service.
- **"Please hold, your call is important to us."** Be careful what you say.
- Increasing quality and efficiency in your back office increases customer satisfaction.
- If you must use scripts, train your reps to say Please and Thank You, and not sound like a robot.
- Leverage social media. Engage your customer.
- Make it easy for your customer to pay. Accept credit cards and other mobile payments, such as Apple or Google.

"Never ruin an apology with an excuse."
~Benjamin Franklin

Tip 5

**Bookkeeper, Accountant, CPA, PA, EA, CFA
(What's the difference and who do I need?)**

On your team you will need someone to keep the books, analyze and prepare financial reports, and advise on tax and investment matters. Knowing the different functions in the accounting process and the associated responsibilities with each can assist you in selecting the right person or persons.

1. Bookkeepers: Process, record and maintain the financial records of the company. This includes such day-to-day activities as posting and processing payments, purchases, sales and receipts.
2. Accountants: Oversee, analyze and interpret the financial condition of the company.
3. Enrolled Agents (EA) are experts in tax law and can represent individuals or entities in front of the IRS if audited.
4. Certified Public Accountants (CPA) have passed a state exam and are subject to annual continuing education. They can provide all of the above services, including signing financial statements and conducting audits.
5. Certified Financial Advisors (CFA) will help you design and implement an investment strategy based on desired goals.

The Team in Your Corner

- A tax preparer is not always a tax advisor. A tax advisor provides expertise in income taxation matters.
- Make sure your tax advisor is your tax preparer. That way they will apply the tax advice to the tax return.
- As for an Estate Attorney, we often don't think about what happens after we are gone. Plan for the transfer of ownership of your business and assets after your death. This can minimize taxes, costs and above all protect your love ones.
- A financial advisor will recommend and advise on particular investment strategies.
- NOTE: When choosing a financial advisor, ask them how they are to be paid for their services. Beware of commission based fees. They might not be in your best interest.

"You are the master of your destiny. You can influence, direct and control your own environment. You can make your life what you want it to be."

~ Napoleon Hill

Tip 6
Having More Month at the End
of Your Money

Paying bills (expenses) is not as much fun as collecting money. Setting up an Accounts Payable system is a way to track expenses in advance of paying for them (a form of credit). Creating checks and balances in this process will increase efficiency, establish credit, manage cash flow and increase vendor relationships.

1. Establish price, payment and delivery terms up front with your vendors before purchase.
2. Ask your vendors to send statements. Verify individual invoices for accuracy.
3. Run an aging report. Know which invoices are due and when. Manage cash flow.
4. Create systems and controls to prevent internal FRAUD such as check tampering, fraudulent reimbursements and vendors.
5. Separation of duties. One person processes invoices and checks and another person reviews and signs the checks.
6. Pay with credit card. Depending on billing cycle, another 10 to 25 days of leverage. Paying with cash or check? Ask about a discount. You never know unless you ask!

Vendor Relationships

- Pay your vendors on time. If the shoe were on the other foot (your customers were not paying you) what would that be like?
- Communicate with vendors if you are unable to pay in a timely manner. Tell them what you WILL DO, not what you can't do.
- Keep your promise, keep your credibility.
- Open incoming mail immediately. Do not ignore bills, IRS notices, etc. It will cost more if not handled in a timely manner.
- Establish business credit (See Tip 7). It bridges the gap between money in and money out (AKA CASH FLOW).
- Set up automatic payments for recurring expenses such as utilities, phone, credit cards, etc. Your bills will never be late and it saves on postage.
- Ask your vendors to report your good credit.
- Finally, pay all sales, wage and withholding taxes in a TIMELY manner. This money is not yours. Your business, your home and your livelihood depend on it!

"Insanity: doing the same thing over and over again and expecting different results."
~Albert Einstein

Tip 7
Business Bank Account

In choosing a bank, ask yourself: Do I need a face-to-face relationship or can I conduct most transactions online (EFT, Bill Pay, ACH, Mobile Banking, E-Statements, etc.?). Determining your needs up front will help you select a bank that will not only support your business now, but in the future.

1. Establish a relationship with the manager or president who has lending authority.
2. Apply for overdraft protection. Doesn't hurt to prepare for an emergency or a clerical error.
3. Maintain the minimum balance in your checking account. Avoiding fees is like earning interest.
4. Download and store offline your bank statements. Most banks store for only 3 years.
5. Have your bank statement's closing date be at the end of the month. This makes bank reconciliation much easier.
6. Include images of checks/deposits with your bank statements. Perform monthly reviews by scanning signatures and payees for forgery and irregular vendors.
7. Use ACH (direct deposit) for paying employees and vendors. Writing checks is old school.

Establishing Business Credit

Building business credit can be simple, but it takes time. Having access to funds for growth, emergencies or protecting your personal credit is important. Waiting till you need it can be too late.

- Create a separate legal entity (Tip 1).
- Obtain a Federal Tax ID number or EIN.
- Use a mailing address other than your home to protect your privacy.
- Create a business credit profile. Obtain a free D-U-N-S number ASAP.
- Open a business checking account. Name must match legal entity.
- Open a business savings account. Use as collateral for a commercial loan to start your business credit profile.
- Obtain a business credit card. Use strictly for business. NO COMMINGLING.
- Open vendor accounts that report to the credit bureaus. If they don't, ask them if they will.
- Pay all bills on time. Pay early and increase your score.
- Get a domain name for your business, email address and website.
- Get a business phone number and list with 411. Use a virtual number and forward to your cell or home.

"Expect the best. Prepare for the worst. Capitalize on what comes."
~Zig Ziglar

14

TIP 8
Risk Management
Just Fancy Words for Insurance

If you thought bookkeeping was tedious, try understanding insurance! It might be easier to learn Greek than to understand insurance: GL, workers' compensation, auto, property, causality, E&O, BOP, fire, flood, theft, weather and alien abduction. In fact, you can probably buy insurance for just about anything!

1. Insurance is just a type of risk management.
2. It is identifying, analyzing and transferring a potential risk in order to minimize loss.
3. Four ways to minimize loss or risk:
   a. Reject the job, project, offer, customer or contract as being too risky. Simply, DON'T DO IT.
   b. Accept the job, project, offer, customer or contract, but mitigate potential problems by implementing programs: safety classes, health and wellness, training and education courses, etc.
   c. Transfer the risk to someone else through the use of an assignment, agreement, contract, purchase order, etc.
   d. Transfer the risk to the insurance company in exchange for a fee or premium.

Annual Insurance Checkup

- Review your commercial coverage every year. Things change.
- Make sure your employees and your business are classified under the correct workers' compensation and general liability classification.
- Receive discounts for implementing employee training, wellness and safety programs.
- Prepaid premiums add more discounts.
- Bundle products or coverage.
- Increase deductibles.
- Shop around. Not all insurance agents or insurance carriers are created equal.
- Ask if you meet or exceed the BASE policy premium. Often you can add additional coverage until you reach the minimum premium.
- Ask your agent the "What if this happens" question. See HOW and IF the insurance will pay out.
- Closing up business? Talk to an insurance professional. You might be at risk for future claims, lawsuits, etc.
- Know your business better than anyone else. Don't leave it to the insurance agent to guess.

"Success is going from failure to failure without a loss of enthusiasm."
~Winston Churchill

Tip 9
Hiring Employees

Understanding federal, state, and local employment laws can be very complicated. Whether you DIY or outsource your payroll, here are a few things that are mandatory and failure to comply can result in large fines and lawsuits. Start by creating a **New Hire Checklist.**

1. Complete Form I-9 to verify the employee's identity and eligibility to work in the U.S.
2. Provide ACA (Affordable Care Act) Notice to inform the employee of the availability of the Health Insurance Marketplace.
3. New Hire Reporting. Employers must report new hires to their state.
4. Complete FormW-4. This determines how much federal tax to withhold.
5. Understand federal and state wage/hour laws.
6. Know the difference between an Employee and an Independent Contractor. You will avoid substantial penalties and fines.
7. Federal and State Poster requirements. Order FREE at www.dol.gov.
8. Consider outsourcing. Payroll tax law is complicated and mistakes are costly.

Essential Human Resource Policies

- Hiring forms. New hire checklist.
- Job descriptions and classifications.
- Employee and company handbook.
- Work schedule/hours.
- Holiday, sick and vacation time.
- Overtime.
- Timekeeping and payroll frequency.
- Leave of absence.
- Breaks and lunch time.
- Employee benefits.
- Performance reviews.
- Disciplinary actions.
- Workplace health and safety.
- Attendance and punctuality.
- Appearance.
- Conduct standards.
- Use of company property.
- Computer usage policy, including internet, social media and email.
- Personal cell phones.
- Documentation and privacy.
- Reimbursable business expenses.
- Termination.

"America is the land of opportunity. Everyone can become a taxpayer."

~Unknown

Tip 10
Legal Department
(Oops, We Don't Have One!)

While it might not be cost effective to have a legal consultant on staff, being proactive vs. reactive can help your company avoid some common legal pitfalls. Not to mention, it will save you money, protect your relationships and build you a solid foundation for success.

1. Form a legal business entity. (See Tip 1).
2. Get it in writing. Nothing personal, this is business.
3. Do not rely on internet sites or family members for legal advice, forms or contracts. **One Size Fits All** rarely applies here!
4. Customers: Set terms and conditions up front by clearly defining expectation for payment, delivery, returns and refunds.
5. Vendors: Establish price, payment and delivery terms before you purchase.
6. Employees: Establish company policies, procedures and create an HR resource guide. Avoid unnecessary lawsuits.
7. Careful what you say. Understand internet marketing and advertising laws.
8. If in doubt, consult a professional.

Things to Ask Your Attorney

- Ask for a FREE initial consultation.
- Ask about their experience or expertise with the type of services you are seeking.
- Prepare a list of questions. Use the internet to help research and understand your problem or situation; it saves time and money getting down to the nitty-gritty with your attorney.
- Set ground rules. Communicate your expectations.
- Ask for their rate sheet.
- Ask about paying by the service rather than paying by the hour.
- Ask about a standard contact or template that can be used versus creating one from scratch.
- Ask if the paralegal can help. A bit cheaper!
- Review the bill.
- Establish partnership and shareholder agreements. Never again get entangled in the "he said, she said" trap.
- Copyrights, patents and trademarks? Better now than later.
- Do not chit-chat with your attorney, unless you do not mind paying $300 per hour. A shrink is cheaper and makes better sense!

"Make it idiot-proof and someone
will make a better idiot."
{Unknown}}

20

Tip 11
Cyber Security

Your computer is at risk of a break-in. Keeping your software up-to-date is critical. While no security system is 100% foolproof, taking some very simple steps can keep a hacker away.

1. Frequently update your software, including your operating system (Microsoft & Mac) & plug-ins (JAVA, Adobe Reader, Flash, etc.)
2. Most software updates provide security fixes and features.
3. Install Antivirus/Malware Software. This provides protection against attacks by ZOMBIES, Trojans, keyloggers, spyware, adware, ransomware and children.
4. Set to update your antivirus software daily. Scan system hard drive at least once a week.
5. Back up your DATA. Use both an external hard drive and online storage system.
6. Use strong passwords. A password manager system will track and store them.
7. "Turn ON" your Firewall. Think of this as your computer's personal security guard.
8. Turn your computer off. Harder to break in and REBOOTING can fix problems.
9. Secure your wireless router (SSID). Change the default password, encrypt your data and stop broadcasting your presence to everyone.

READ BEFORE YOU CLICK

There are dozens of ways your computer can become infected with spyware, malware or other viruses. To provide an additional layer of protection, follow these simple guidelines:

- The Pop-up made me do it! Most problems occur by simply NOT reading or understanding what you are clicking on.
- Beware of FREE downloadable software. Can contain Adware (pop-ups that are annoying and sometimes dangerous) and Scareware (false advertisements that your computer is infected with a virus).
- BE WARY of email attachments. If not expecting it, do not open it.
- Phishing scams attempt to steal your personal information by **imitating** trusted sources, such as your bank. Scrutinize emails that solicit sensitive information, passwords, etc.
- Watch out for "ZIP" files in emails. They are most likely traps.
- Avoid websites that require you to log in through an email link. Go to the website directly.
- Watch out for bogus websites. Look for the "security lock" and prefix https:// in the address line.

"Passwords are like underwear. You don't let people see it, you should change it very often, and you shouldn't share it with strangers."
~Chris Pirillo

Tip 12
Show Me the Money

Accounts Receivable is money owed by customers in exchange for products or services delivered, but not yet paid for. Extending credit can be risky and have a huge impact on your company's cash flow. Understanding the rewards and risks can help you decide.

PROS
1. Increases sales.
2. Enhances customer relationship, loyalty and repeat business.
3. Competitive advantage over competition.

CONS
1. Decreased cash flow. Company obligations must be met through other sources of capital.
2. Establish credit policy: Contract terms, conditions, credit application, credit check, and compliance with FTC (Federal Trade Commission).
3. Risk or cost of a customer slow-paying or not paying at all.
4. Increased recordkeeping: invoicing, calculating late fees and collection letters.
5. Cost of legal action or lawsuit for non-payment.

Maintaining Customer Relations

- Establish credit policy.
- Check your customer's creditworthiness. Look at trade references. How much credit is already being extended?
- Set appropriate credit limits. Start small.
- How will you handle returns, refunds or money-back guarantees?
- Will you be able to collect late fees and attorney fees?
- What happens if your customer goes out of business?
- Email invoices and statements ASAP.
- Create and review your AR aging report.
- Follow up by phone if payment is late. Don't wait until it gets out of hand.
- Accept credit cards. This shifts the risk to the credit card companies. To prevent charge backs and holds, find a dedicated merchant processer who is familiar with your type of business.
- Consider early payment discounts. Minimal cost, but increases cash flow.

"You will get all you want in life, if you help enough other people get what they want."
~Zig Ziglar

Tip 13
The P's and Q's of Email Etiquette

Email is the most common form of business communication, quickly replacing the formal business letter. Unfortunately, we often forget some of the most basic common etiquette, creating a cringe-worthy, WRONG first impression of your company.

1. Use a professional tone, be courteous and respectful. Avoid slang, text talk and yelling (using CAPITALS).
2. Use formal greetings and closings until you have established a relationship. Going from "Dear Mr. Smith" to "Hey Bob" too fast can burn the relationship before it gets started.
3. Please and Thank You. So simple!
4. Write your subject line first before composing your email. It should convey exactly what is inside.
5. Keep the email short and precise. If your recipient is prioritizing, your email might not get read.
6. Don't rely solely on spell check. Proofread for grammar, content and clarity.
7. Acknowledge receipt of email. A simple **Got it, Thanks, or I'll be in touch** will do.
8. Use an email address with your name in it; less chance of it landing in JUNK Mail.

Email Tips and Tricks

- Get a domain name and use a professional email address. Yahoo, Gmail and Hotmail can be easily hacked.
- Type your email content first before typing in the recipient name. Less chance of sending prematurely before you EDIT mistakes.
- If sending large attachments, ZIP IT or spread it out over several emails. Large files jam things up.
- Sending marketing or sales emails without permission is SPAM. Besides being annoying, it might be against the law!
- Set a 1-2 minute delay on your outgoing emails. This gives you a chance to retrieve an email before going out, especially if you suffer from "trigger finger" syndrome.
- Do not rely on email if your message is urgent or you require an immediate response. Pick up the phone.
- Do not send confidential information by email. It can be hacked or forwarded by mistake. Who knows where it will end up!
- When an empoyee leaves your company, don't leave their emails in limbo. Forward them to the appropriate person.

As for REPLY ALL, think twice. Albert Einstein said it best: "The difference between stupidity and genius is that genius has its limits."

Tip 14
The Customer Service Experience

"A customer is the most important visitor on our premises; he is not dependent on us. We are dependent on him. He is not an interruption in our work. He is the purpose of it. He is not an outsider in our business. He is part of it. We are not doing him a favor by serving him. He is doing us a favor by giving us an opportunity to do so." (QI August 2, 2012)

Statistics show that it costs companies 6-7 times more money to find new customers. Return customers are known to spend more money than first-time buyers, so increase your bottom line by providing an exceptional customer experience.

1. Train your employees. Invest in them.
2. Acknowledge the customer. Be accessible, knowledgeable and helpful.
3. Remember, anything less than good service is bad service.
4. If you are having a bad day, guess what? Your customer will too!
5. Thank your customer. They have choices.
6. Reward returning customers for their continued patronage.
7. If you do not know the answer, say so and set a time to get back to them. Do not make promises you cannot keep.

18

Avoiding Customer Pet Peeves

- Customers waiting in long lines at checkout may experience **Buyer's Remorse** and put the items back.
- When opening a new checkout line, take the next person, not the last person.
- Count change back to your customers. This simple action is not only courteous, but it ensures accuracy for both parties.
- If you ask your customers "**Did you find everything you were looking for?**" and they answer "NO", be prepared to assist them. Why ask, if you don't intend to offer help.
- Do not put a phone caller in front of the live person in line.
- Shopping for an advertised product only to find there are none.
- Addressing your customers with dear, honey, or sweetie pie might seem harmless. Keep those "terms of endearment" for your loved ones, not complete strangers. Address your customers respectfully.

"Your most unhappy customers are your greatest source of learning."
~Bill Gates, Microsoft

Tip 15
Exit, Stage Right or Left?

Creating an exit strategy while in the process of building and growing your business seems rather foolish. However, at some point every business owner will exit. Will that be on your terms or on someone else's? Just like Snagglepuss, will that be exit, stage right or left? You decide.

1. Are your business goals in alignment with your personal goals?
2. Are you creating passive income to provide for retirement?
3. Are you creating a business to sell and maximize investment return?
4. Are you creating a legacy to pass on to your love ones?
5. Have you considered life and/or disability insurance to protect and ensure your business continues if the unexpected occurs?
6. Partners? Do you have agreements in place if you or your partners want out?
7. Have you consulted an estate attorney regarding potential income and estate tax?
8. In the event of a forcible exit or bankruptcy, consult an experienced attorney.
9. Building a saleable, transferable or willable business requires planning. **It takes time**.

Exit Ideas and Options

- Quit – Close up shop and liquidate assets.
- Find an apprentice. Fresh ideas.
- Find an investor. New capital.
- Find a manager or partner to operate your business, making it more desirable to sell.
- Develop systems and tools to duplicate yourself, thus making you obsolete in your business.
- Sell to a larger company or merge with a similar one.
- Keep it in the family. Create a legacy.
- Sell to your employees. They know the company sometimes better than you.
- Keep ownership, create passive income.
- Hire a manger and enjoy time off.

> *"The wise man bridges the gap by laying out the path by means of which he can get from where he is to where he wants to go."*
> *John Pierpoint Morgan*

You've finished. Before you go…

Tweet/share that you finished this book.

Please star rate this book on Amazon.

Reviews are solid gold to writers. Please take a few minutes to give us some itty bitty feedback on this book.

ABOUT THE AUTHOR

Karen O'Connor moved to Steamboat Springs, Colorado a few weeks after graduating college with a B.A. in Marketing. She became an official "ski bum" her first year, skiing over a 100 days. She later received her MBA in Business Administration. She is an active business consultant, real estate investor and options trader.

For over 25 years Karen has developed practical financial and operational strategies that enable her clients to grow their business and create a sustainable foundation for success. With extensive knowledge steeped in accounting, finance and project management, she educates business owners on finding the right systems and professionals, thus allowing them to focus on the task of running their businesses.

Karen looks forward to building a legacy of integrity and unparalleled customer care. She continues to gain the knowledge and skills necessary to drive her clients to organizational excellence.

"My passion is helping small business owners and entrepreneurs live theirs!"

BackOfficeTips.com
SuccessExcellerator.com

If you liked this book you might also enjoy...

- **Your Amazing Itty Bitty® Advanced Video Marketing Book** – Gary Howarth

- **Your Amazing Itty Bitty® Book of Quickbooks® Shortcuts** – Barbara Starley, CPA

- **Your Amazing Itty Bitty® IRS Tax Audit Prevention Book** – Nellie Williams, EA

And many more Itty Bitty Books® available on line...